MW01503092

A Crabtree Branches Book

eXtreme SPORTS
Surfing

Bernard Conaghan

Crabtree Publishing

crabtreebooks.com

School-to-Home Support for Caregivers and Teachers

This high-interest book is designed to motivate striving students with engaging topics while building fluency, vocabulary, and an interest in reading. Here are a few questions and activities to help the reader build upon his or her comprehension skills.

Before Reading:
- *What do I think this book is about?*
- *What do I know about this topic?*
- *What do I want to learn about this topic?*
- *Why am I reading this book?*

During Reading:
- *I wonder why...*
- *I'm curious to know...*
- *How is this like something I already know?*
- *What have I learned so far?*

After Reading:
- *What was the author trying to teach me?*
- *What are some details?*
- *How did the photographs and captions help me understand more?*
- *Read the book again and look for the vocabulary words.*
- *What questions do I still have?*

Extension Activities:
- *What was your favorite part of the book? Write a paragraph on it.*
- *Draw a picture of your favorite thing you learned from the book.*

Table of Contents

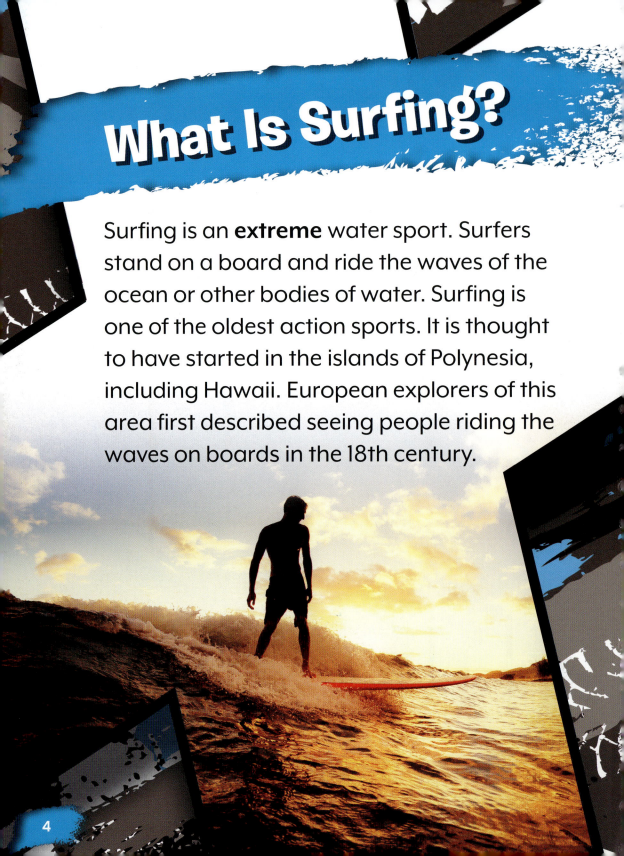

What Is Surfing?

Surfing is an **extreme** water sport. Surfers stand on a board and ride the waves of the ocean or other bodies of water. Surfing is one of the oldest action sports. It is thought to have started in the islands of Polynesia, including Hawaii. European explorers of this area first described seeing people riding the waves on boards in the 18th century.

Fun Fact

The first surfing contest was held in 1928 in California.

Parts of a Wave

In surfing, there are various parts of a wave. The lip is the top part of the wave before it breaks. The shoulder is farther down in the wave and is less **steep**. The face or wall is the steep part of the wave that surfers ride.

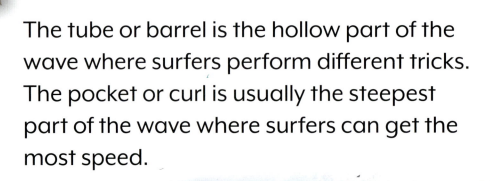

The tube or barrel is the hollow part of the wave where surfers perform different tricks. The pocket or curl is usually the steepest part of the wave where surfers can get the most speed.

Fun Fact

The record for the highest wave ever surfed is 86 feet (26 m).

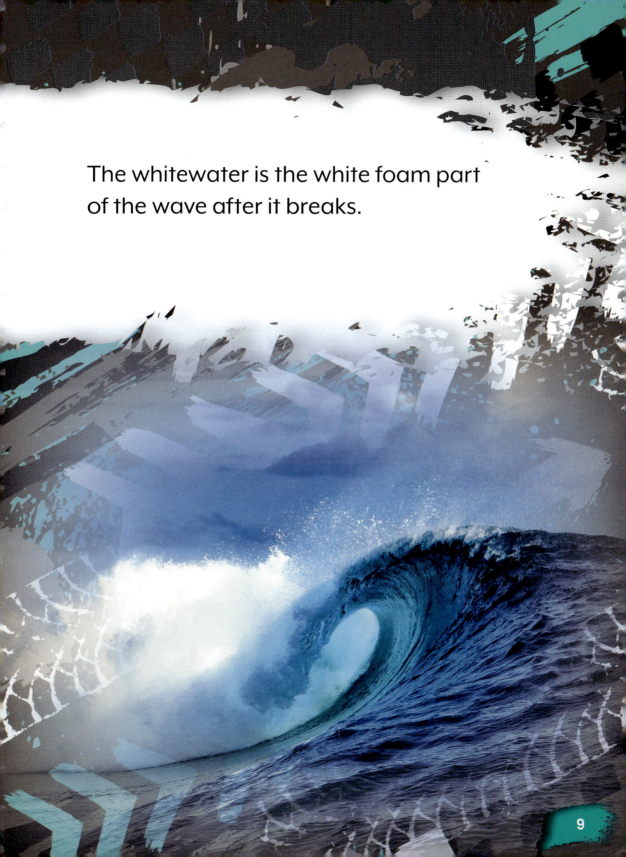

The whitewater is the white foam part of the wave after it breaks.

Surfing in Action

When they enter the water, surfers lie flat on their boards and paddle with their hands. This is how they go out into the ocean and catch waves. **Professional** surfers ride waves and perform different types of tricks.

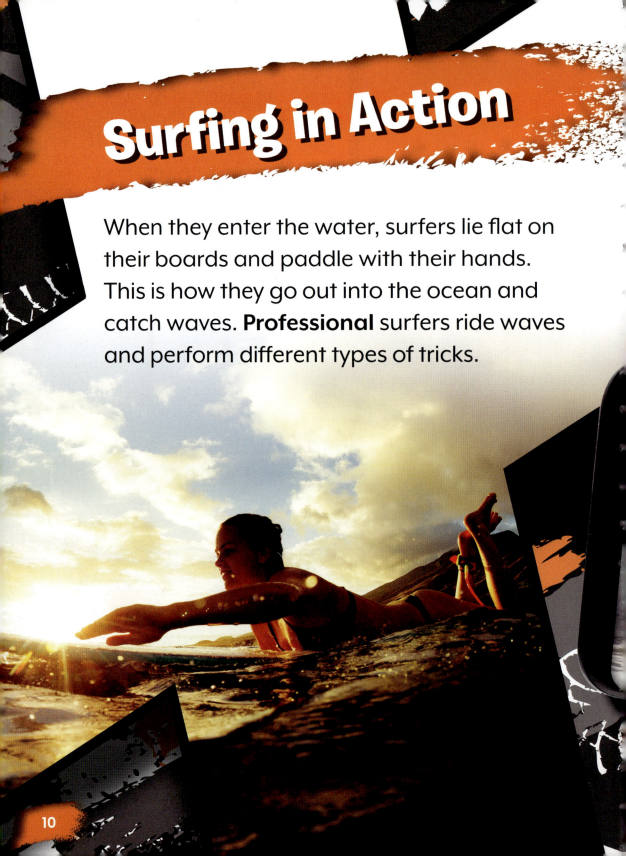

Surfers use the waves to do different types of tricks and flips. This can include using a wave as a **ramp** to do a 360-degree turn in the air. This is known as a 360.

Fun Fact

Joseph Wolfson, or Dr. 360, was one of the first surfers to do a 360 spin.

A 360 is when the surfer launches off the water and does a 360-degree turn with their board while in the air.

The aerial, or air, is another popular surfing trick. In this trick, the surfer picks up speed, soars in the air, and then lands on the face of the wave. This trick was **inspired** by a popular trick in skateboarding called the ollie.

Fun Fact

Flynn Novak created this trick at the age of 19!

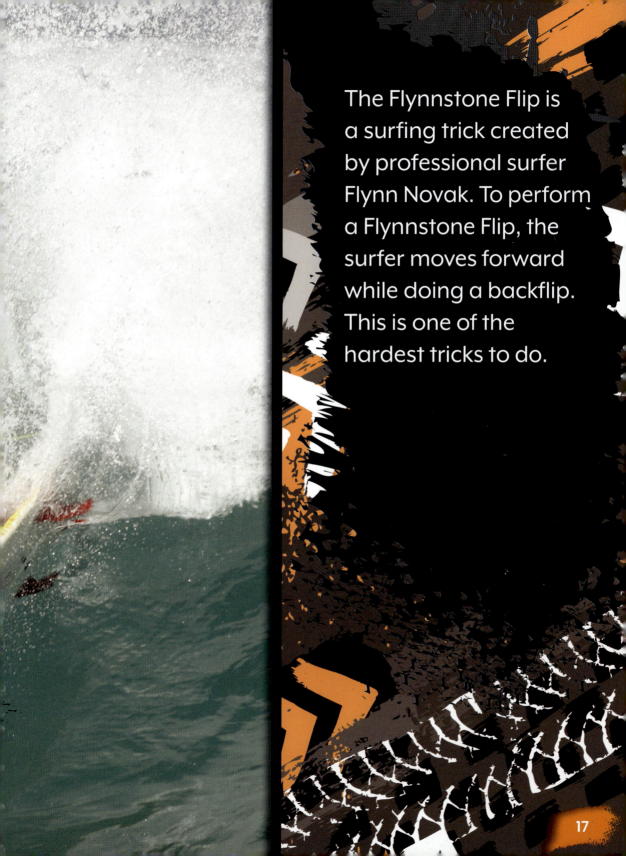

The Flynnstone Flip is a surfing trick created by professional surfer Flynn Novak. To perform a Flynnstone Flip, the surfer moves forward while doing a backflip. This is one of the hardest tricks to do.

Parts of a Surfboard

One of the most important parts of surfing is the surfboard, of course! The front, or tip, of the surfboard is called the nose. It is angled to help the board **maneuver** in the water. The bottom of the board helps it to glide.

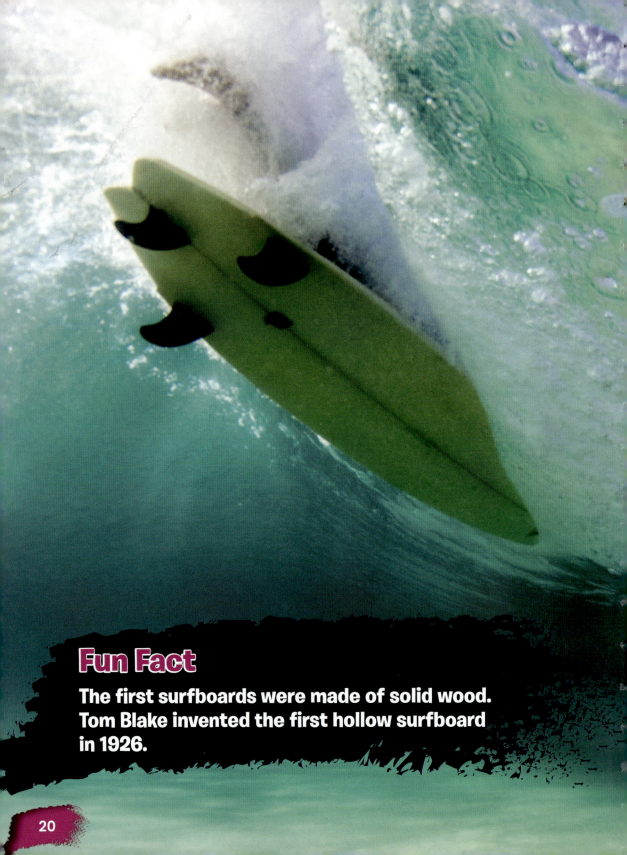

Fun Fact

The first surfboards were made of solid wood. Tom Blake invented the first hollow surfboard in 1926.

The back of the surfboard is called the tail. It is slimmer and sharper than the front. There are different tail styles for different types of waves. The fins are connected to the tail. They help with steering. They also keep the board more stable.

Your Surfing Career

The best way to start surfing is to go out on the water and practice. Getting a coach to teach you the **fundamentals** of surfing can also be helpful. A coach can help train you to compete in surfing events.

The World Surf League, or WSL, organizes professional surfing events. It holds many **tournaments** throughout the year in many locations around the world. The WSL was created in 1976.

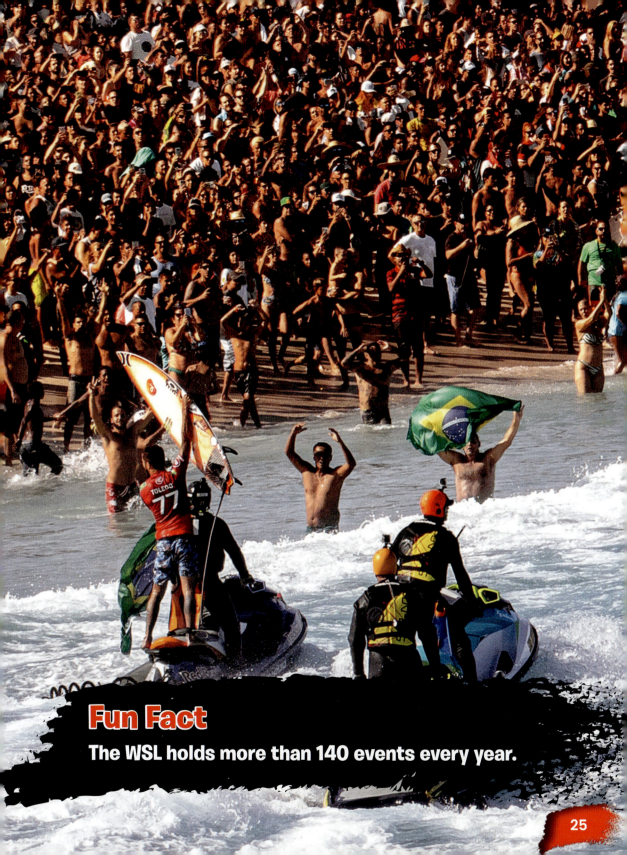

Fun Fact

The WSL holds more than 140 events every year.

Surfing Legends

Throughout the history of surfing there have been many different **legends**. One of them is Kelly Slater. He has won nearly every major record in surfing, including 11 world championships. Slater was born on February 11, 1972.

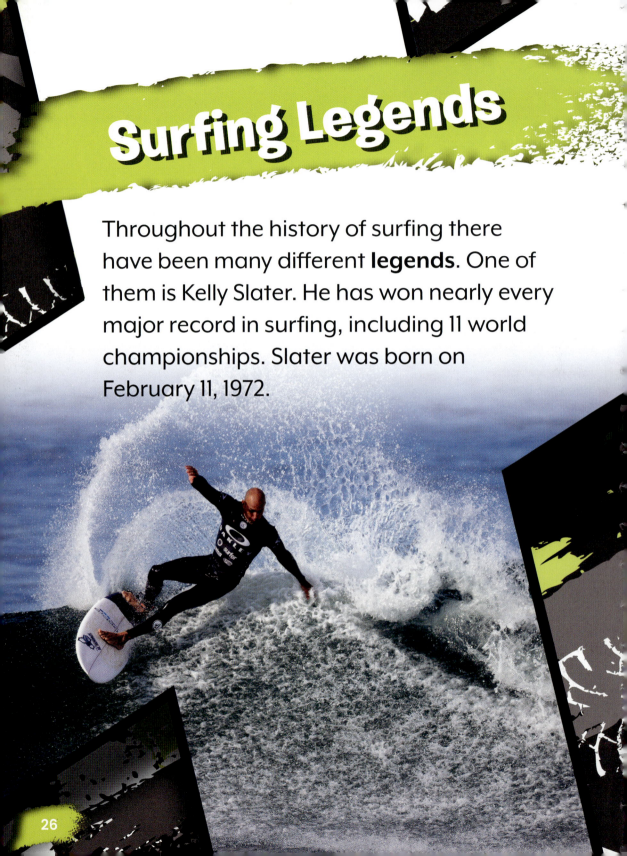

Fun Fact

Slater is both the youngest and oldest men's world championship winner.

Another legend is Stephanie Gilmore. She was born on January 29, 1988. Gilmore has won seven world championships, the first four of them **consecutively**.

Fun Fact

Gilmore is the first surfer to have won the world championship in their **rookie** year.

Glossary

consecutively (kuhn·SEH·kyuh·tihv·lee): Following one after the other in a series

extreme (ek·STREEM): Something that is far beyond the normal

fundamentals (FUHN·duh·men·tlz): The basics of something

inspired (in·SPY·urd): To cause something to be created

legend (LEH·jind): Someone who is famous and admired for doing something well

maneuver (muh·NOO·ver): To move carefully and skillfully

professional (pruh·FEH·shuh·nuhl): Someone who is paid to participate in a sport or activity

ramp (RAMP): A piece of equipment with a slope

rookie (ROOK·ee): A first-year player in a professional sport

steep (STEEP): Almost straight up and down

tournament (TUR·nuh·ment): A competition with many participants

Index

Websites to Visit

www.xgames.com

www.worldsurfleague.com

https://isasurf.org

About the Author

Bernard Conaghan lives in South Carolina with his German shepherd named Duke. Every year he goes snowboarding in Switzerland. He is a coach on his son's football team. He always eats one scoop of peach ice cream after dinner.

Written by: Bernard Conaghan
Designed by: Jen Bowers
Series Development: James Earley
Proofreader: Melissa Boyce
Educational Consultant: Marie Lemke M.Ed.

Photographs: Cover image ©2015 EpicStockMedia/Shutterstock, background ©Matisson_ART/Shutterstock; p.3 © ©2021 Denis Moskvinov/Shutterstock; p.4 ©2015 EpicStockMedia/Shutterstock; p.6 ©2011 EpicStockMedia/Shutterstock; p.7 ©2017 Joel Everard/Shutterstock, phone ©2017 Vasin Lee/Shutterstock; p.8 ©2015 EpicStockMedia/Shutterstock; p.9 ©2019 vladimir3d/Shutterstock; p.10 ©2015 EpicStockMedia/Shutterstock; p.11 ©2021 max blain/Shutterstock; p.12 ©2013 homydesign/Shutterstock; p.13 ©2007 Pedro Monteiro/Shutterstock; p.15 ©2020 Iryna Horbachova/Shutterstock; p.16 ©2008 Mana Photo/Shutterstock; p.18 ©2020 Steve Collender/Shutterstock; p.19 ©2014 Pressmaster/Shutterstock; p.20 ©2018 Taylor Wilson Smith/Shutterstock; p.22 ©2021 Denis Moskvinov/Shutterstock; p.23 ©2020 yurakrasil/Shutterstock; p.25 ©2019 Pablo Almeida/Shutterstock; p.26 ©2015 Brian A. Witkin/Shutterstock; p.27 ©2019 LouisLotterPhotography/Shutterstock; p.29 ©2012 peapop/Shutterstock

Crabtree Publishing

crabtreebooks.com   800-387-7650
Copyright © 2023 Crabtree Publishing

Printed in the U.S.A./012023/CG20220815

Published in Canada
Crabtree Publishing
616 Welland Avenue
St. Catharines, Ontario
L2M 5V6

Published in the United States
Crabtree Publishing
347 Fifth Avenue
Suite 1402-145
New York, New York 10016

Library and Archives Canada Cataloguing in Publication
Available at Library and Archives Canada

Library of Congress Cataloging-in-Publication Data
Available at the Library of Congress

Hardcover: 978-1-0396-9666-2
Paperback: 978-1-0396-9773-7
Ebook (pdf): 978-1-0396-9987-8
Epub: 978-1-0396-9880-2